Christopher John did what was expected of him. He worked hard at school, went to a good university, graduated at the turn of the 21st century and got a job in the city. Over the course of a decade he had his car stolen twice, got mugged, fell victim to identity theft and had his house burnt down. Eventually he moved to Yorkshire for a better life.

Hiking in the country, where he felt much safer, an innocuous looking cut led to septicaemia and immediate hospitalisation. Yet through it all he kept smiling.

CJ is an eternal optimist who believes life is a gift to be seized. Upon discharge from a long stay in hospital, CJ quit his full time job, started writing and founded a coaching company, with the aim of inspiring individuals and companies alike.

In his spare time he can be found in coffee shops and tearooms across Yorkshire.

"*I founded Inspiring Aspiration with only one goal:* **to change people's lives for the better.**

One thing is true, no matter whom I have worked with: only when people are asked the right questions, are they able to come up with their "right answers" – the answers they need to achieve any and all of their aspirations."

Christopher John

Founder of Inspiring Aspiration

**Discover more about coaching
and how it changes lives at:
www.inspiringAspiration.com**

storm
in A
tea cup ?

Develop a positive
outlook on life,
during your tea break

CHRISTOPHER JOHN

iA

This book is dedicated to the woman I love. Without her encouragement and support, all the optimism in the world wouldn't be enough to have kept smiling throughout the trials life has thrown.

But furthermore to anyone who has stared at their cup, wishing they were more awake, wishing it were Friday or wishing for circumstances other than the current ones: hopefully this book alone can make you smile. If I can change your outlook, YOU can change your life.

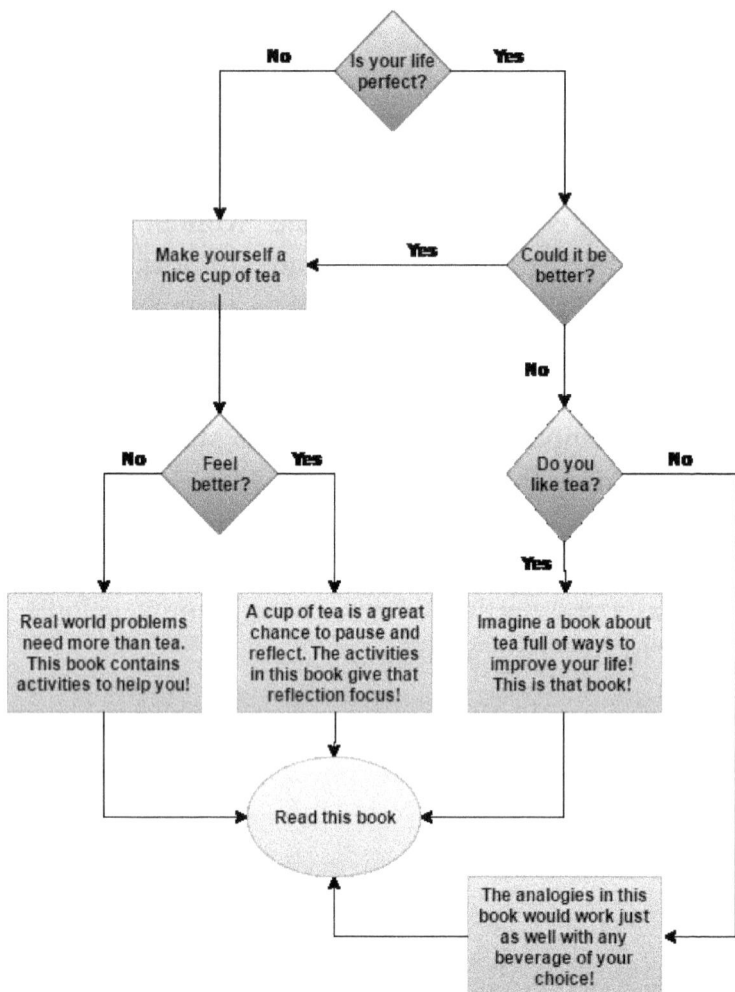

```
                              Is your life
           No                  perfect?               Yes
    ┌──────────────────────────◆◆◆──────────────────────────┐
    │                                                         │
    │                                                         ▼
    │                              Yes                  Could it be
    ▼                      ┌──────────────────────────  better?
Make yourself a           │                             ◆◆◆
nice cup of tea  ◀────────┘                              │
    │                                                    │ No
    │                                                    ▼
    ▼                                              Do you
  Feel                                             like tea?        No
 better?  ◀───────────────────────────────────    ◆◆◆  ──────────────┐
  ◆◆◆                                               │                 │
 No │  Yes                                      Yes │                 │
┌───┘  └────┐                                       │                 │
▼           ▼                                       ▼                 │
Real world   A cup of tea is a great     Imagine a book about         │
problems     chance to pause and         tea full of ways to          │
need more    reflect. The activities     improve your life!           │
than tea.    in this book give that      This is that book!           │
This book    reflection focus!                                        │
contains                                                              │
activities                                                            │
to help you!                                                          │
    │           │                             │                       │
    │           ▼                             │                       │
    │      Read this book  ◀──────────────────┘                       │
    └──────────▲───────────────────────────────────────┐             │
               │                                         │             │
               │                              The analogies in this   │
               └──────────────────────────── book would work just ◀──┘
                                              as well with any
                                              beverage of your
                                              choice!
```

Is your life perfect?
- No → Make yourself a nice cup of tea
- Yes → Could it be better?

Could it be better?
- Yes → Make yourself a nice cup of tea
- No → Do you like tea?

Make yourself a nice cup of tea → Feel better?

Feel better?
- No → Real world problems need more than tea. This book contains activities to help you!
- Yes → A cup of tea is a great chance to pause and reflect. The activities in this book give that reflection focus!

Do you like tea?
- Yes → Imagine a book about tea full of ways to improve your life! This is that book!
- No → The analogies in this book would work just as well with any beverage of your choice!

Real world problems need more than tea. This book contains activities to help you! → Read this book

A cup of tea is a great chance to pause and reflect. The activities in this book give that reflection focus! → Read this book

Imagine a book about tea full of ways to improve your life! This is that book! → Read this book

The analogies in this book would work just as well with any beverage of your choice! → Read this book

Contents

Introduction

The vast majority of readers are going to fall into one of two main categories:

1) You love storms, tea and/or teacups.

2) You want to develop a positive outlook on life during your tea breaks.

If you do not fall into these categories, I would question whether you read the title before picking this book up, but welcome you regardless.

The purpose of this book is to work with your current outlook on life and make you think in a way that will make your life better. With identical intentions to making you a cup of tea, I wish to make you happier, content and satisfied. I wouldn't make you coffee if you asked for tea, and I wouldn't force Earl Grey upon you because I believe it is a better brew. Similarly I don't want you to think entirely differently to the way you currently do now. There will be those of you who are risk-averse and those who are mavericks in your field. Some of you may spend your life planning for the future, others who live from one day to the next. I hope I find readers among the pessimists and the optimists. There will be those who claim to be realists, but are put firmly in one camp or the other by their colleagues. Similarly there will be other readers who flirt between the two camps in different aspects of their lives. Whatever your outlook in life, I don't want to change you; I want to work with you.

The most common analogy for different outlooks on life is the cup half full and/or half empty. The analogy fails when the pessimist (claiming the cup is half empty) claims to be a realist by pointing out that quite literally the cup is indeed half empty (they're not wrong). The same could be said of the optimist. Erm... end of analogy. I realised the extremists of optimism would claim their cup is full no matter how much you pointed out the liquid was an inch below the rim. To them, the cup will be full to the brim. We all know these types of people – they are a blessing to the workplace and their friends – always smiling, always cheery.

So what is your outlook? Is your cup full to the brim, or is it completely empty? Most likely, it falls somewhere in between. In this book, we will stretch this analogy to breaking point (quite literally in chapter 15). Every reader will be able to identify with the current state of their cup, which if we are honest will change from one area of our lives to the next. Whatever frame of mind you are in, I want you to be able to make progress towards the one goal we all share - a better future, one in which you are happy.

If your cup is always full I want you to harness that optimism to achieve goals bigger than some people dream. The pessimist will find a way to overcome the obstacles you just assume will present themselves. Whatever your outlook on life, there will be times you need to stop, have a cup of tea, and think about the way forwards. Like the leaves in our teapots, ideas need time to brew. By following the activities at the end of each chapter, you will take steps towards that better future - a positive future.

Before we go on, I feel I must address those of you who are reading for the pure love of tea. When I chose the title for the English edition of this text, I was faced with a vast multitude of possibilities. It appears the British love their tea and we love the crockery that tea is served in. The English language is overflowing with tea and teacup based idioms:

Storm in a teacup
Not my cup of tea
For all the tea in China
Their cup flows over

Then there are a whole host of idioms we can use over the meal that is afternoon tea:

A lot on their plate
Can't have their cake and eat it
Takes the biscuit
Spinning plates

Finally we have the classic:

Their cup is always half full

I have lived in both the North and the South of England, indeed my family are a mixture of the two, and I seem to have an equal proportion of friends and family who say either my "cup" is half full or my "glass" is half full. I'm not going to lose sleep over it. I could have written this book purely from the analogy of a glass. I didn't. I wrote this book fuelled by tea. I discussed it with my editor over tea. I imagine you and many million readers like you will read it with a cup of tea... and yes, that statement was said with the sheer optimism of an author whose cup is always full!

However full your cup may be, I will now let you enjoy this book. Turn to the chapter that suits your current state of mind, or read through in order. Try all of the activities in this book, or just those necessary for your current situation. However you use this book, I hope it provides you "food for thought" and helps you develop a positive outlook, but more importantly a smile.

Storm in a Teacup?

<u>The Cups</u>

The following section of this book contains 15 different outlooks on life and related thought exercises and activities. Readers may wish to read through this book in order and complete each activity as they discover them. Other readers may relate to particular exercises and wish to complete them on a regular basis. Both approaches have their own merits, but greater wisdom and self awareness will develop from dedicating an appropriate amount of time to completing the activity at the end of each chapter.

Your cup is full to the brim

This was how this book started. I ordered a cup of Darjeeling, and it came to me full to the brim. Being British I would never have complained had I received anything less, even if I was anything less than gruntled; when I order a beverage, I want a full cup.

I don't of course. When you make yourself coffee, tea or indeed any drink at home, do you ever fill it to the brim? I doubt it. You would spill it. You seriously can have too much of a good thing. A cup full to the brim is too full... most of the time. When it is brought and put before me, then sometimes it is nice to overindulge.

I realised there was a key difference between full, and what we mean when we say full. If we couldn't agree what full meant, no wonder we can't decide between half empty and half full. I shall come to that matter in time. Realising there were so many perspectives of my teacup, my head was suddenly full of ideas to write about outlooks on life.

Well, not full as such.

Many of you may know the anecdote about the jar full of pebbles, sand and tea*. It reinforces the notion that full can mean different things. The question is: how full do you want your life to be?

Just as a cup full to the brim will easily spill over, if we fill our lives with everything on offer, there's a risk we can't handle it all. So you may wish for more money, fast cars and fame, but what if these things pushed out the things that matter? That isn't to say we can't handle a fuller life. I'm not telling you to learn to settle for less. Just as in a café I treat myself and I am served a full cup.

At home however, I consider my cup full when it still has space to slosh around, because that is what happens. Life sloshes us around and we need space to manoeuvre. At home I am content to be in my cosy couch, with my battered slippers, and be around people I love. This to me is "full"filment.

---

* See Appendix 1

If your cup is full to the brim, you may often find there is so little room for manoeuvre that you do spill things, or have to sacrifice one aspect of your life for another. It may be useful to you to spend time realising your own priorities.

Activity 1

PLEASE READ APPENDIX 1 BEFORE FOLLOWING THESE INSTRUCTIONS:

- First make a list of all the things you think you *need* in your life.
- Now take three pieces of paper (or one piece of paper split in three) and label each "golf balls", "pebbles" and "sand".
- Proceed to write the things from your first list on the appropriate piece of paper, or section.
- Place the list or lists somewhere you see them often, and whenever faced with conflicts of interest, try to prioritise the "golf balls" over the "pebbles" and "pebbles" over the "sand".
- Now, drink some tea

Your cup is full

When we make ourselves a cup at home, we don't fill it to the brim. In truth, even the steadiest hand would likely spill it if we did*. I will safely assume that all of us can accept we say a cup is full even when by the most literal definition it is not.

A theatre full to the rafters actually only has its seats filled with a vast empty chasm between them and the aforementioned roof (necessary for acoustics) – but only tea based analogies are allowed in this book, so forget that for one moment!

My point in case is that lives don't have to be full to be full. We don't notice the empty part of the cup if we consider the liquid inside to be a quantity considered enough to be full. Similarly if you consider what you have in this life to be full, you will not notice any lacking. More importantly you won't be spilling the important bits!

---

* In 2012, Rouslin Kretchetnikov and Hans Mayer won the Ig Nobel Prize in Fluid Dynamics for their study of liquid sloshing in a cup carried by a walking person. Basically, they validate my above point.

In the previous chapter we considered the need to prioritise the things in our life so when spillage was necessary you chose the right priorities for you (don't let anyone else decide them for you). The difference here is not prioritising one aspect over another, but actually not noticing something you do not have, and still considering your life as full.

The only way to focus purely on the full bit is to be happy with the full bit. Often we try to fill our lives to the top because we're not happy with what we already have. If this is the case we certainly need to evaluate what is already there. I know when I am served a bloody good cup of tea, I'm too hasty to have a sip to concern myself with how close it is to the top.

To be happy with a full cup that isn't full to the brim, try the activity on the next page. It helps you identify exactly what you want your life to be full of by discarding the rest: in real life terms – ignoring the little empty bit.

Ultimately we need to learn what it is in life that makes us feel fulfilled. It is important to feel our life is full with many of the things we already have. Unhappiness is often caused by the absence of things we feel we want or desire.

Activity 2

An activity to reinforce our appreciation of the things we truly are fulfilled by is to write down all the things we want to BE, to DO and to HAVE on lots of separate pieces of paper. Following this, write down WHY we want these things. If we cannot justify these wants (and saying "it will make me happy" on its own is not justification), scrunch the pieces of paper up.

If you want to whittle your list down further, pick up two pieces of paper at random. If you were forced to choose between the two, which would you choose? Throw away the other piece of paper.

In this way we can quickly see what matters to us. This will be different for all of us. The important point now is to not try and fill your life with the things you do not consider a priority at the expense of those you do.

Your cup is nearly full

Whoop whoop! Your cup is nearly full. Let us clarify "nearly full" as anything over half full (more on what that means in the next chapter). This incontrovertibly means you have lots of tea in your life. In the previous chapters we have discussed balancing our priorities when our cup is literally full and realising it doesn't have to be up to the rim to truly be full. In this chapter, despite having a nearly full cup, we do need to acknowledge that there's a bit of tea missing. Now while you may feel we are being the opposite of positive by focussing on that absence, awareness can lead to improvement.

Activity 3

Imagine the scene - you are making a cup of tea for a guest. You've topped up their cup from the kettle and haven't managed to fill their cup. There isn't time to boil the kettle again, but you are aware of the emptiness. How can you improve their tea drinking experience to make up for the less than full cup? Come up with as many ideas as possible before continuing...

What did you come up with? Biscuits on the saucer, a wafer balanced on the rim, a sprinkle of undissolved brown sugar on top?

What I'd like to draw your focus to in this chapter is the awareness required to improve a situation, sometimes called the 0.2 second rule. For many of us there is nothing in our lives that would matter if they were 0.2 seconds slower, it is just too small to be significant. When Usain Bolt broke the 100m world record for the first time in 2008, the time difference between himself and Richard Thompson in 2nd was 0.2 seconds. The difference between 3rd and 4th (i.e. getting a medal or not) was only 0.02 seconds! There are many fast runners in the world, there is only one Usain Bolt. With focus and practice many of us can become good at something in a number of years. It is that extra 0.2 however, that will make us truly great, and that can take a lifetime of discipline and dedication.

What are you good at? What would you need to do to be great? Acknowledging our cup is nearly full is the first step, but maybe it will never be full unless we get up out our seats, and do what needs to be done to fill the cup! You need to want a full cup; you need to be prepared to do what it takes to fill it.

Apparently it takes 10,000 hours to master something. Anecdotal evidence can be found in the time the Beatles spent in Hamburg before their first record released back home. Performing and rehearsing for up to 12 hours a day between August 1960 and December 1962 would come to a total of 10,440 hours. After all that practice, what happened next?

10,000 hours is a lot; it is full time dedication for nearly two and a half years, "half-time" dedication would make it five years. That time will pass anyway, so how much time can you dedicate to attaining your goal?

Activity 4

Take a piece of paper and answer the following:

- Think about your current goal. How much time are you currently dedicating to it?
- Where could extra hours be found and what would you have to do to dedicate this time to achieving your goal?
- How can you make this time habitual?
- How are you going to remain motivated?

Your cup is half full

As I dangerously wade into this age old debate, I must point out your cup is half full and half empty. The optimists and the pessimists are both right, but who is happier?

Let us consider how much half is. Half of most things are quite acceptable. Imagine someone paying half of your mortgage off for you. A team who scores half of the total goals in a match never loses. Your other half is quite a wonderful person in their own right. In most circumstances, half of anything is a pretty decent amount and while I am sure there are examples to the contrary, why point them out?

Let us return to the cup. If someone offered you a beverage in the morning, but said...

"we're short on milk, are you okay with half a cup?"

...then I am nigh on certain most of us would accept the half cup rather than go without. Just think of it as a smaller cup if you must, then poured into a larger cup.

In the real world, many people's cups are half full and half empty. Put simply, the half that is full of drink represents all the good in your life, and the half that is empty can be thought of as the things you are missing.

It is too simplistic for the optimists to tell the pessimists to focus on the things they have, but similarly the pessimists cannot deny the things they have and a stalemate is reached.

It is the realist who says the cup is half full and half empty. They appreciate the things they have, and aspire for the things they do not. To improve our reality, we must be realists.

Realistically you may say the things you want are far greater than the things you have and thus the half full, half empty analogy is inaccurate. But do not just think of material gain. Consider all of your skills and your experience. These are the things you have which will actively facilitate you attaining the things that you want.

Just as a half empty cup must have a half that is full, every negative has a positive. The following activity will help you view both in the most appropriate way for progress.

Activity 5

Take a piece of paper and write down five things in life you are not happy with. Now take another piece of paper and write down the same five things, but remove any negativity. For example...

"I am too fat and need to lose 5 stone"

could be written as:

"I am only 5 stone away from my ideal weight"

The first statement starts life as a rather negative fact that you have set in stone, whereas the second statement becomes a point of progress, expressing a measurable goal and reinforcing the ever changing nature of all things.

When you have rewritten your statements I suggest throwing away any negative statements. Similarly, if you're not happy with a half empty cup, why not take a big swig, and get yourself a refill!

Your cup is nearly empty

I'm not going to argue with you that your cup is nearly empty; I'm simply going to point out that you still have a cup of tea. How empty does a cup of tea have to be to no longer be a cup of tea? You have a cup, it has some tea in it and therefore you have a cup of tea.

We will later discuss the size of our cups, for it could be argued if we poured the contents of this cup in a smaller cup, we would once more have a fuller cup. Feel free to argue that you don't want a smaller cup. Say that out loud and you might worry that you sound privileged or precocious. This more than any other chapter is about perspective. While a half empty cup doesn't require a different perspective to be seen as half full (as one literally implies the other), a nearly empty cup is going to require you to focus on what you do have to be seen as positive.

I appreciate fully, if it were as easy as choosing to be positive, you wouldn't need a book of tenuous analogies to help you do so, but revisit the above point. In a smaller cup this amount would be more than full. Do you want to be the person who tells the world you deserve a bigger cup than others?

You're still here, so I can assume you want to see the positives when they're limited. It isn't easy. There is a certain irony in our insistence to compare ourselves to others. You want the bigger car, the bigger house, the easier life. The fact that you crave these things (and there is nothing wrong with that, indeed it is the fuel of ambition), means you are aware of their existence. You know others have easier, better, or more acclaimed lives. It isn't fair, and you want what you don't have.

The fact you can read or the fact you currently hold a book (even more so if an eBook) means you have more than most and you know it. I hope you are able to eat well, and have a roof over your head; others do not. But you weren't comparing yourself to those folk were you? So are you comparing yourself to others or not?

I am sorry your cup is nearly empty, but there's so much gravity in the casually thrown statement "it could be worse". If you want to compare yourself to others acknowledge the full position, for every negative, you KNOW there are positives. If you can view yourself in isolated objectiveness, credit to you, please tell me how. Viewing things from other perspectives is hard. It's a skill that needs practice to develop. It requires imagination, vision and speculative hypothesis, but will give you much greater insight into any situation.

Activity 6

This activity will require quiet reflection. Give yourself the appropriate time to carry it out.

YOU: Think through any situation you are currently facing in life. Write down how you feel. To facilitate this consider what you can see, hear and even smell. Imagine being in that very situation right now.

THEM: Now write the same situation down from the view of someone else involved in that situation. Write things down as if you were this person. Refer to their experiences in first person, and yourself as him/her/them. Be as thorough as you were for your own feelings.

OTHER: Finally imagine an observer watching your interaction from afar. Write down what this person is seeing and hearing. Again write in first person.

Your cup is empty

Is it?

Look at the cup carefully. Does it look empty to you? There are clearly the remnants of our last drink, still tepid. Before you interject, the next chapter will address the completely empty cup. In life however, it is rare we have a completely empty cup, because we will always have the experiences of what has gone before us.

In the case of our cup, we've all done it – taken our last swig, sat for a few moments and then noticed the remnants have pooled at the bottom and gone for one last sip. This is particularly effective for milky beverages. Other times, we've considered the cup empty, but the person who made the brew for us is offended, as they believe we are leaving a bit. We'll discuss perception once more in a later chapter, but for now let us accept that if a cup isn't completely empty there is value in the remnants.

If you're thirsty, one last sip is appreciated.

If it's gorgeous, one last taste brings pleasure.

What are the remnants of our last brew in life? They can be a multitude of things, but let us think of them as the things we don't usually consider but can help us make progress. This may be the contacts in our diary we haven't contacted in years, or more figuratively the skills we haven't used since our student days or a previous career.

I'm not going to be the fussy host who insists you finish every last drop. However, if your cup is empty and you don't know what to do, acknowledgement of these remnants can make all the difference.

You've asked everyone in the company and no one knows how to save that contract? Is there a business card at the back of your diary from someone who knows someone? You've emptied your bank account and need more money for your rent? Is there something in the loft you could sell?

Basically, when you appear to be at the bottom of the cup of possibilities, it is time to consider those remnants as a blessing. Keep sipping, scrape the last foam out with your spoon, even sip the spillage from your saucer, but do what is necessary to quench your thirst.

Activity 7

This will help you access those skills you may only call upon when you feel your cup is empty. You have a goal, and you've exhausted all options (or maybe just want more options).

- Take several pieces of paper, the larger the better. Write on each one a skill you wouldn't normally use, but that you may have used in the past. An example may be "Team work" if you are a sole-trader, but were part of a sports team years ago. Try to write at least 5 of these.

- Place these pieces of paper on the floor around you. Stand in the middle and choose one previous skill to focus on. Step out onto the piece of paper and talk aloud about how you demonstrated this skill in a previous situation.

- Now turn around and look at the middle, visualising your current situation. Again, speaking aloud, state possible ways to use this skill in your present goals.

39

Your cup is completely empty

So your cup is completely empty.

If we take another viewpoint it is completely clean. It is a blank cup of possibilities. There is nothing in it. We have nothing to wash out and can put anything we like in it without the hint of contamination from previous beverages.

What a rare opportunity it is to be presented with. In fact let us not think of it as being given an empty cup of tea. The gift here is clearly not a beverage, but a cup. Can you tell the difference between a clean, empty cup and a new cup?

If you were at a friend's house and they gave you an empty cup, saying *"help yourself to a drink"* what would you choose? You would go to the cupboard, and look through the beverages on offer. Sure you normally have tea or coffee at home, but now you are presented with camomile and peppermint and what on Earth is Lapsang Souchong?

If we truly have choice, it makes us think...

In real life it is so rare we are presented with a completely empty cup, completely new opportunities, without a hint of past experience. Maybe we have won the lottery, or maybe work has relocated us abroad where nobody knows us. Of course, we often refuse to start afresh because we don't want to let go of the past, but in truth there is little preventing us starting afresh with a clean cup.

So many of us get up, go to the same job in the week and do the same things at the weekend. There is nothing wrong with this. I wonder how many of us however, do this because we feel we do not have a choice. We feel that way because no one is presenting us with a choice. No one is asking us on a daily basis to help ourselves to a drink. But help ourselves is exactly what we must do if we want change.

If every day someone asked you what you wanted to do today, you might do something differently. So ask yourself! If you want a clean cup, apply for a job a hundred miles away, or a thousand miles, or two miles.

You can of course choose your usual drink. You may like doing what you're doing. So choose it. Just remember, you always have a choice.

Sometimes it is impossible to plan ahead without mentally taking your baggage with you. Instead let us work backwards from a ripe old age, at which we have completed our life goals.

Activity 8

- Imagine yourself sat on your porch, your patio or in your garden. You are old but happy, having lived a long and happy life. Imagine a grandchild, great niece or just a friend asking about your life. Tell them all of the things you have completed that have made you happy and content today. You may want to write these things down, in past tense:

  "I once climbed Mount Everest"
  "I wrote a book, and people bought it!"

- Now here's the hard part. What changes do you need to make in your life to achieve these goals? Do you need to start with a clean empty cup? You may not, but if you were presented with one, what choices would you make? What's stopping you making these choices now?

Your cup is stained

This chapter has the potential to divide a nation, but most likely in to a vast majority and a small minority. To the minority group, I know you like a stained cup or pot, there's nothing wrong with a bit of tanning. To you this cup is merely ready for topping up. Either reread the last chapter or move onto the next. For the vast majority of you, a stained cup is not a pleasant experience. Sure, it's a completely empty cup. You've done the last activity, and you want to fill it up, but you feel whatever was in there last is holding you back from doing so! What if it taints the taste, affects the flavour?

Let us be honest, whatever was in there last was probably put there by you. It was probably enjoyed by you previously. It is only now that you want a new cup, that you feel the previous cup now serves you no purpose and is holding you back. Do you regret having the previous cup of tea? Probably not. Is it now time to wash the cup? Most definitely.

In most kitchens, we don't need to wash our cup immediately after using. There are other cups. Similarly in life, we rarely need to resolve our issues instantly. Work can provide respite from an argument with a partner; the weekend can provide respite from an argument with a colleague. However, if you never rinse your cup out, one day you will go to get a cup and find the enjoyment of the next drink is severely compromised.

You have several choices:

1) Wash your cup immediately upon completion – resolving issues in life immediately may not always be your choice, but when it is do you seize it?

2) Get in the habit of washing several cups from time to time – in life this will mean finding time to reset certain situations: time away with the family you don't see in the week or finding time to socialise with colleagues away from the stress of the office.

3) Wait till there is no acceptable cup and do something about it – just as this will be stressful if you're desperate for a brew, allowing issues in life to build up may lead to an inability to deal with them down the line.

We tend to get dragged down and overwhelmed by things that accumulate over time. Just as we won't rinse the cup every time, we don't have to discard everything in our life that may hold us back, but we do need to be aware of them.

Activity 9

It is important to identify what you're tolerating. Make a list of as many things as you can think of that have accumulated in your cup. Examples may include incomplete projects, guilt, bad habits, and unresolved issues. Write down anything that's surfaced in your life and will eventually need dealing with, just as at some point the cup is going to need washing.

Now you are aware of these issues, you can't leave them unresolved forever. Great news however, you now have a to-do list and a lot of built up stain broken down into manageable chunks. Choose one to begin working on. It may be the easiest one to resolve (the least stained cup) or it may be the one you are most worried about (the REALLY stained cup). Regardless, just wash one cup at a time and soon you'll have a clean cupboard of cups.

Your cup cannot be found

You have no cup.

If you have bought into the analogies in this book so far, then you are simply going to have to accept that the cup is not there. I chose not to put it there and only I know where it is. Sorry dear reader if I have caused you distress.

There will be times in life you need a cup. There will be times in life you do not know where a cup is, but somebody else does. In such circumstances your only option is to ask. In such circumstances, the most important decision will be to ask the right person, and this does not have to be the most obvious. If you were round my house, you may wish to ask me where I keep my cups. If however, you did not wish to appear incapable of finding your own cup, you may ask someone who has been to my house before. Maybe you would ask an acquaintance of mine, or maybe just someone who has found cups in the past.

Knowing who you can ask and who you can trust is vital in planning for the future. Just as Rome wasn't built in a day, it wasn't built alone.

It is speculated that the average person meets more than 10,000 people in their life. Today's habit of collecting friends on social media has highlighted just how many bit-part actors play a part in our lives. However, it is the meaningful relationships in our life that shape our experience. The limit of these relationships is known as Dunbar's number and is accepted at around 150*. It would be difficult to dedicate time to maintain any more than this.

If you were to list every colleague, family member and friend, could you happily cull off enough to get your number to 150? Such a practice may seem brutal or callous. It is probably easier to build up a list of *allies* – a list of those people in your life who help you move towards your goals, whether they be personal fulfilment, career enhancement or greater experience of life.

The most important "exercise" you can do to build up a list of allies, is giving others a reason to be your ally. The following activity should help you:

- Realise your allies
- Maintain those relationships
- Consider the relationships that serve no purpose

---

* See Appendix 2

This exercise is best completed alone and kept private. It can be a powerful and enlightening activity, but should not be carried out in groups, nor rarely shared due to its personal nature.

Activity 10

Create a brainstorm of people who are your natural allies – people who would help you in times of need and move you towards your goal. It may be useful to group people by the following categories:

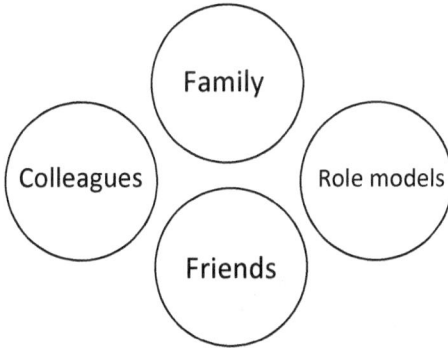

For each person you add, make sure you can think of a reason to maintain the relationship.

For each person you write down, think of the reason or reasons they would add you to their brainstorm. If you can't think of anything now, make sure you give them a reason in future.

Your cup belongs to Schrödinger*

Has anyone ever made you a hot drink, and then for one reason or another, you think you have tea but they made you coffee or vice versa? On that first sip, the brain does the strangest thing. No matter how much you love tea and coffee, if you taste the unexpected, your brain hates it!

Let us rewind just a matter of seconds. You were sat in your friend's house, and they made you a lovely drink. At this point you were sat with a refreshing cup of tea. Of course you also had an invigorating coffee, but you didn't know this yet. You were happy and all was right with the world.

Fast forward a minute or so. You have politely informed your friend that you are perfectly happy with coffee. Your taste buds and brain have had a quick conference call and come to terms with the situation. You are happy and all is right with the world.

---

* Schrödinger's Cat is an experiment by Erwin Schrödinger, in which a cat is placed in a sealed box. Without opening the box, one cannot know if the cat is alive or not. Through the medium of quantum physics, he explains the cat is both alive and dead until the moment of opening. See Appendix 3.

You may be able to see where I am going with this. If only we could rewind and fast forward, we could see that everything was and always will be all right, if we can just configure our brains to the present! The unexpected and the unknown are always our worst pain and biggest fear. Being aware of that is the first step to coping with it.

I want to emphasise the necessity to cope rather than conquer the unexpected. One can never be completely prepared for the unexpected; the unexpected by its very nature is not something we are prepared for. We can minimise the possibility by being prepared for a multitude of hypothetical situations, but we will still need mental strategy to cope when we are not prepared.

So how do you cope with the unexpected? The thought exercise that follows will develop creative areas of the brain to facilitate original thought in original situation. Ultimately, it is a question of giving your brain time to think, to catch up and analyse BEFORE your reaction. So often we react before thought. Saying "OW" before any pain manifests itself may only provide embarrassment, but what happens if you react with anger in a work environment?

When life throws something at us we haven't experienced before, we need to think differently to how we have thought in the past. However, creative thinking is not a basic skill that can just be called upon. While some claim creative thinking is "right-brain" and "non-linear", in time it can become habitual, using all parts of our brain – requiring logical, linguistic thought and stimulating reactive motor control. The only way we can develop this is with regular practice.

Activity 11

Find time at least once a week to answer a purely hypothetical question. Dedicate this time to creating the most thorough "solution" possible. Appendix 4 contains a list of 9 questions, but here are a few to get you started:

- What would I do if I found out a colleague was stealing company property?
- If I desperately needed money and knew I would not get caught, would I steal?

Discuss your answers with a friend and argue your point. Convincing yourself is key to developing your thought process.

Your cup's contents have been decorated

Some people love it, and others hate it, but nearly every coffee shop in the land takes pride in doing it. The contents of the cup have been perfectly brewed and poured, and then the server adds their own unique flourish. You're not likely to find it on a mug of builders' tea, but order a Chai Tea Latte and I can almost guarantee it*.

Why do establishments decorate the top of our cups? One would think it is simply to look good. It IS to look good. A "good looking" brew suggests a quality beverage and demonstrates the skill of a barista. There is nothing wrong with taking pride in one's work, nor demonstrating this to the world.

When I put this to Ellie, a barista of many years, she agreed, but was quick to point out that great decoration also demonstrates the correct density of foamed milk. In other words it serves a purpose.

Just because we didn't know the purpose, it didn't stop us appreciating the art. Do we need purpose for everything in our lives?

---

* Coffee drinkers among you will get this on almost every drink they order - another reason to stick to tea!

We are living in a material world, and whether we like it or not, we are material girls (don't argue with me boys). Look around and count the physical objects that make you happy. Even if we disregard the ornamentation of our lives – the jewellery and flashy cars, we still take pleasure in "necessary" objects: clothes, furniture and the houses we live in.

Which of our material goods serve a purpose in our lives? Let us use the example of our clothes. Clothes have been worn almost the entirety Homo sapiens have walked the planet. They provide warmth and protection, which occupy the first and most basic step of Maslow's hierarchy of needs*. They can also give us status, esteem, and impress others – even attracting a mate. Could they land us our dream job, or business deal? In this sense they can fulfil many needs. So are clothes material goods?

We all have needs. We also have desires, and these desires can motivate us to achieve great things. In such a way, a desire for a Ferrari can be the catalyst for greatness. Don't be ashamed of materialism but be aware of it so you don't chase dreams for the sake of it!

---

* See Appendix 5

Motivation is powerful but elusive. Many of us rarely stop and ask the reason for our actions. When we have a "why" however, we will find our actions are easier to complete, and more satisfying. A powerful tool for finding and maintaining motivation is to create a vision board.

Activity 12

- Decide on a physical or digital vision board.
- Collect pictures of your goals to put on it.
  - Look through magazines, blogs or search for specific desires you have.

The act of collecting these images serves to remind you of your "why". You work hard to earn the Audi; you pull all-nighters to deserve that dream holiday. Finding pictures for your desires also helps you analyse your material needs versus your internal desires – what picture will you use to represent "comfort" or "a loving family life"?

Put your board somewhere you will see it regularly. Talk about it with colleagues and friends, and keep it updated to keep your motivation as high as it needs to be to live the life you "need".

Your cup is a mug

Why do we drink from mugs? A quick brainstorm may result in many things, from it being nice not to bother with a saucer to they are better for warming both hands.

Ultimately mugs are about comfort - a steaming mug of tea by the fire, a mug of tea during your break, and even (heaven forbid) the comforting mug of soup*. No one in their right mind would argue against the elegance of drinking from a proper cup, but when we need a brew sometimes only a mug will do.

We have our favourite mugs and it doesn't matter that the mugs in our kitchens don't match; mugs are a familiar staple in all cupboards. Mugs are apparently the 2nd most popular "destination-themed souvenir" after t-shirts. You can even buy gimmick mugs such as in the shape of a Rubik's cube. For some of you this wouldn't be comfortable, and here we have found the boundaries of your comfort zone.

---

* I am well aware of the famous brand that is almost synonymous with the general product that is "Cup-a-Soup". I guess "Mug-a-soup" just didn't have the same ring, but I'm yet to meet anyway who has made such a soup in an actual cup.

In life we cling to our comfort zones. We aspire to spend our lives in them. Most of our working life is spent trying to make them more comfortable. Even those of us who spend years bungee jumping in foreign climates are often more comfortable doing so than returning home to get a job in the city.

The issue you may have with your comfort zone is when your goals lie outside of it. The job that would give you the lifestyle you desire may require you doing things you have never done before. Travelling may require you to let go of financial security. The great thing about comfort zones is that when we stretch ourselves, we can expand the limits of our comfort, pulling those goals into an area we are comfortable attaining. I call this the "Stretching Space" – the activities in life that we may feel uncomfortable completing now, but help us to grow.

There is a point beyond the stretching space and I call it the "Point of Panic". Often we attempt to stretch ourselves, but go so far from our comfort zones we panic. Going here won't help us grow, but instead will have us retreat further into our comfort zones. Instead of getting closer to our goals, we are now further than ever. The activity that follows can help avoid this situation.

Activity 13

Step 1: Draw three concentric circles, with "comfort zone" in the centre circle, "stretching space" in the middle circle, and "point of panic" in the outer circle[*]:

Step 2: Place current goals in the comfort zone, stretching space or point of panic. Are they attainable with a little stretching, or far out of reach?

Step 3a: For goals with a little stretching write down the skill you will need to stretch a little to attain it.
Step 3b: If the goal is in the "Point of panic", try to place an intermediary goal in the "Stretching Space" to aim for first and repeat step 3a.

---

[*] A blank diagram can be found in Appendix 6

Your cup is made for espresso

Your cup is indubitably full. Full to the brim in fact, but let us not explore that topic again. You order espresso*, you get a full cup; you are happy; the world keeps on going.

But wait! How would you have felt had you received such an amount in a regular sized cup? You may claim you would understand, given the potency of such a brew, but then why do they bother to serve espresso in these cups in the first place?

The answer is of course, perspective and perception. We are humans, and rightly or wrongly, to us size matters.

While it may be more economical for cafés to buy in bulk one size of cup, for sure customers would complain when they received their thimble-full of espresso at the bottom of a large cup. Even giving them a slightly larger espresso cup, only three quarters full, would result in their chagrin.

It is not the volume of liquid the customer cares about, but their belief of what is and isn't acceptable. Are they fussy? Are we any different?

---

* I'm not quite sure why you didn't order tea.

Our perception of our lives is based upon a set of beliefs. If I made you a cup of tea in an espresso cup, no matter how I argued you had a full cup, you would argue that it was a small cup. This is because you have a belief that teacups fall within a certain size range, and this belief has been reinforced with years of tea drinking.

Many beliefs are harmless or useful. Other beliefs are limiting. For example, in 1953 no one believed it was possible to run a mile in under 4 minutes. The evidence was simply that no runner had ever done so before. On May 6th 1954 Roger Bannister ran one mile in 3 minutes and 59 seconds; his record lasted only 46 days. Today, over 50 years later, sub-four minutes is now seen as the standard for any middle-distance runner to reach.

Do you see how the belief in 1953 had overwhelming evidence (there was literally no evidence to the contrary), but this was far from proof it was not possible.

What would you like to achieve in life, but you currently believe is impossible? It is important to question the evidence.

For the next activity we are going to challenge any one of your limiting beliefs.

Activity 14

Draw a circle in the middle of your page, and four additional circles connected to it, one above and below, and one on either side*. Begin by placing a limiting belief in the centre and giving 4 pieces of evidence that support the belief. I have used the example that I make poor tea.

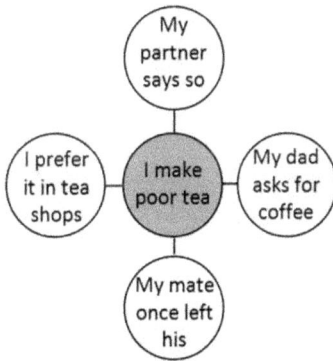

For each piece of evidence, write down three questions to challenge it. For example for the evidence *"my partner says so"* we would question what my partner's qualifications were for judging tea, what were their standards for good tea and what were their intentions in declaring this to me.

---

* A blank diagram can be found in Appendix 7

Your cup is upside down

The cup is upside down. To demonstrate an upside down cup, I contemplated using a photo of an upright cup turned the other way up. In fact, how do you know I didn't? Of course the perspective looks the same as other pictures, suggesting the cup is indeed upside down, on top of a saucer. Could the saucer be said to be on top of an upside down cup? Memories of Paul Daniels' 'cup and ball routine' may spring to mind for the older reader[*].

Admittedly I discussed perspective in the previous chapter, but in that situation we had a reference point. We knew that was a smaller cup, and for our circumstances it was full. Now we can't even be sure which way round the cup is, so we can't possibly ascertain its size. Maybe this cup is full. The saucer prevents us knowing.

When nothing is familiar to us we are back in childhood. Don't be confused, be curious. Don't be worried, be in wonder...

---

[*] For anyone not familiar with Paul Daniels, or indeed the aforementioned routine, I recommend looking it up online.

How can we see things in a way we have never seen things before? To literally "see" things activates the occipital lobe of the brain, but MRI research has shown that imagining the sight of something stimulates the occipital, frontoparietal, posterior parietal, precuneus, and dorsolateral prefrontal regions of the subjects' brains! In other words, when we imagine something, we cannot help but use all areas of our brain that process and analyse all of our senses. Our imagination cannot "see" things alone. In this way our imagination is as powerful as real experience.

Working this backwards, if we regularly stimulate these same areas of the brain required for touch, sight, smell, taste and hearing, we can empower our imagination to think up more and more original thought. Research has shown a greater imagination helps develop a greater sense of empathy, enhances your own memory, and can lead to greater self esteem.

In life, seeing things from different perspectives is essential. This doesn't mean "a different perspective from your own", it means being able to have several different perspectives at the same time, and choosing the one that works for you.

Imagination has no real limits, but given it is a product of our own thoughts and experiences, the more experiences we have, the greater resources we have for original thought. The easiest way to see things from a fresh perspective is to put yourself in a position you have never been in before.

Activity 15

Exercise 1: See how long it takes to complete the following checklist:

- Work in a different part of the office for a day
- Travel home via a different route
- Sleep on the opposite side of the bed
- Get a drink from a café you've never visited
- Speak to a stranger
- Listen to a new radio station

Exercise 2: Using the above checklist or the longer list in Appendix 8, try to complete every item on it once a month (or week if you're feeling brave).

Exercise 3: Set a friend or family member a challenge by making each other a list of a set number of items. How many new experiences can you have?

Your cup is broken

Oh no!

What happened?

Who knows? Apart from the person who broke it. You may have broken it. Maybe it was someone else.

Before you become exasperated at the futility of a chapter questioning such a hypothetical situation, please admit you have indulged in such speculation yourself. I'm not pointing a finger, we all do it. Something goes wrong in our life and we want to apportion blame. When there is no apparent culprit, we speculate.

In the case of the broken cup in this chapter, who broke it is irrelevant. In the case you have a broken cup in your cupboard, the same is true. Quite simply, the broken cup will not hold a brew, thus it simply will not do.

You have choices: fix it, get a new cup or go without tea. No other options are available!

In life, things break all the time - #SadButTrue.

Relationships break down, our health can fail us, jobs and contracts have termination clauses. Often things break because of neglect (see the cup is stained chapter for discussion on maintenance). Other times things just run their natural course. Knowing which has occurred is not easy in life, but that doesn't mean you shouldn't think about it. People in breaking relationships may say:

"Let us just see if things work out"

But if there is one thing I can assure you, it is that things do not just work out. They are fixed or remain unfixed. There is a cause and an effect.

Returning to the question of who broke the cup, it is irrelevant, but that does not mean we can ignore the breakage. We fix it or we discard it. There has been a cause, there is a current effect, next comes our reaction.

In life you must accept that everything happens for a reason – the reason being that somebody made it happen.

Activity 16

To help decide how to move forward you are going to draw a lifeline – a timeline of the decisions you have made, and the ones you need to make.

Step 1: In the middle of a large piece of paper put your current situation:

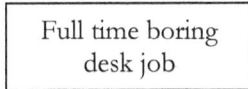

Full time boring desk job

Step 2: Work backwards, put the major decisions you had to make that led to this:

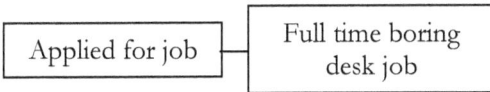

Applied for job	—	Full time boring desk job

Step 3: At the far right write where you want to be:

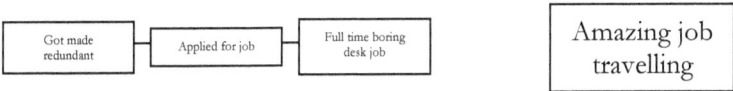

Got made redundant	—	Applied for job	—	Full time boring desk job		Amazing job travelling

Step 4: Begin to fill in decisions you are going to have to take to reach your goal:

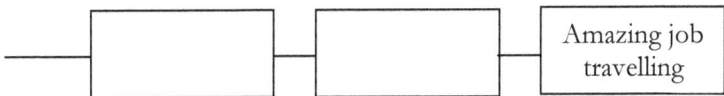

—|	|—|	|—| Amazing job travelling

75

Storm in a Teacup?

Making the Tea

In 1946 George Orwell published an article in the Evening Standard *discussing the 11 issues he deemed most important in making a cup of tea. In this short section there are 11 important issues and many more questions every reader should ask themselves, regularly if possible. Deciding upon the answers may not lead to the perfect life, just as no one can decide upon the requirements for the perfect tea, but dedicated time to reflection upon them will lead to a difference much more noticeable than putting the milk in first or after the water! This section contains nothing but questions. You contain all the answers.*

Where does the tea come from?

"What are the values you will never compromise?"

Are you proud of where you come from? Does your life reflect your geographic and cultural roots or is it a product purely of your own experiences?

In what quantity should I make my tea?

"If you had unlimited money, what would you do?"

How much money do you need to achieve your goals? Is a finite amount of money enough? How will you know when it is enough?

Should I warm the pot first?

"If there was one thing you wish you had begun 5 years ago, what would it be?"

If 5 years ago you had began piano lessons, or saving £10 a week, what difference would it make to life now? In 5 years time what one thing would you like to have started today? What is stopping you?

How strong should the tea be?

"How do you know how strong you are? What do you or can you do that tests your strength?"

How often do you shy away from something through fear or fear of failure? What would you do if you knew you had the strength to succeed? How can you know your strength without trying?

Does tea go in bags, a strainer or loose in the pot?

"If you could travel anywhere, where would you go?"

Are you bound to where you currently live? Would travel add value to your life? What is preventing you travelling?

Do I stir the tea in the pot or the cup?

"What issues in your life need resolving now, and what are you tolerating but need to resolve later?"

When is your life going to be how you want it to be? Why are you waiting to achieve certain goals?

Take the kettle to the pot or pot to the kettle?

"Who can you go to, to help you in this situation?"

Do you need to go to them, or will they approach you? What do you need to do to get help? If you knew someone could help you, why wouldn't you ask for help?

What should my cup look like?

"How do other people see you and how do you wish to be seen?"

Are appearances important to you? Are appearances important in any part of your life? How can you change the way you are perceived?

Milk or cream?

"What are the things you want but don't need?"

How will the things you want affect your life when you obtain them? Are there things you need, that you are not currently working towards?

One lump or two... or none at all?

"What habits are having a negative effect on your life?"

What are you doing on a daily basis that is moving you further from your goals? What can you do to break these habits? What actions can you take to move you towards your goals? How can you make these actions habits?

Should I put the milk in first or last?

"Will you begin living the life you want when all your goals have been achieved, or will you need to begin living that life to achieve them?"

What will your life look like when your goals have been achieved? What parts of that life can you start living now? What is preventing you living in some ways right now?

Storm in a Teacup?

Summary of activities

1: Help deciding priorities
2: Removing unimportant desires
3: Imagination exercise
4: Analysing how time is spent
5: Turning negatives into positives
6: Viewing life from other perspectives
7: Harnessing unused skills
8: Visualising a life to be proud of
9: Removing things you are tolerating
10: Making natural allies
11: Considering hypothetical situations
12: Creating a vision board for motivation
13: Moving beyond your comfort zone
14: Challenging beliefs holding you back
15: Experiencing new things
16: Drawing a timeline of your life

Storm in a Teacup?

Appendices

These appendices serve to give greater value to the reader. This may be through expansion of ideas discussed briefly in this book, or by providing extra material for the activities at the end of each chapter. Either way, no appendix found its way into this book by default, and it is hoped that where the reader has related to a particular "cup of tea", the additional material in these appendices will facilitate further thought and possible progress.

Appendix 1: Filling the jar of life

A teacher stood before his class and had some items in front of him. When the class began, he picked up a very large and empty glass jar and proceeded to fill it with golf balls. He then asked the students if the jar was full. They agreed that it was.

The teacher then picked up a jar of pebbles and poured them into the jar. He shook the jar lightly. The pebbles, of course, rolled into the open spaces between the golf balls. He then asked the students again if the jar was full. They agreed it was.

The teacher picked up a box of sand and poured it into the jar and of course the sand filled up everything else. He asked once more if the jar was full. The students responded with a unanimous yes.

The teacher then produced a cup of tea from under the table and proceeded to pour the entire contents into the jar, effectively filling the empty space between the grains of sand. The students laughed.

"Now," said the teacher, as the laughter subsided, "I want you to recognise that this jar represents your life. The golf balls are the important things - your family, your partner, your health, your children, your friends, your favourite passions - things that if everything else was lost and only they remained, your life would still be full. The pebbles are the other things that matter, like your job, your house, your car. The sand is everything else - the small stuff.

"If you put the sand into the jar first," he continued, "there is no room for the pebbles or the golf balls. The same goes for your life. If you spend all your time and energy on the small stuff, you will never have room for the things that are important to you. Pay attention to the things that are critical to your happiness. Play with your children. Take time to get medical checkups. Take your partner out dancing. Play another 18 holes on the golf course.

"There will always be time to go to work, clean the house, give a dinner party and fix the guttering. Take care of the golf balls first - the things that really matter. Set your priorities. The rest is just sand."

One of the students raised her hand and inquired what the tea represented. The teacher smiled. "I'm glad you asked. It just goes to show you that no matter how full your life may seem, there's always room for a cup of tea."

Appendix 2: Dunbar's Number

Prior to Robert Dunbar's research in the 1990s, primatologists had observed that social groups of primates required individual members to maintain personal contact with all other members of the group. While this century has seen more and more human relationships develop purely online, most of us would agree that our "real" relationships either have more meaning, or certainly a different effect on our lives than our "digital" relationships.

Through extrapolation of data based on the size of the neocortex* in different primates and humans, anthropologist Robert Dunbar hypothesised his limit on the size of social groups in humans at approximately 150.

It was reported in 2007 that the Swedish tax authority reorganised their company to work in offices of no more than 150; this concept had been tried for some time, most famously by the company behind Gore-Tex, W. L Gore and Associates. The company now has over 10,000 staff, which means working out of at least 67 separate buildings. The

---

* The part of our brain most influential in learning and memory

company seems to know what they are doing when it comes to their social policy though, having ranked in the "100 Best Companies to Work For" list published by Fortune magazine, every year since 1984. This year (2016) they were 12th.

Dunbar's number, based as it was on the study of primates, may seem disjointed from our modern day "social networks", connecting people through Twitter, Facebook and other similar sites. The companies who run these virtual communities however, are aware of the implications. Such websites now use algorithms to avoid flooding users with information from hundreds of users and focus on a manageable number. Similarly these algorithms can ensure the money-making posts are the ones we are processing on a daily basis.

The limitations of the human brain to identify with increasingly large social groups may also be playing a part in creating apathetic or worse, bigoted factions of society. A greater understanding of social interaction will be necessary in an ever connected world.

Appendix 3: Schrödinger and his cat

Erwin Schrödinger is known as the father of quantum mechanics, a subject far beyond most of us. That is because it is full of complicated things like the Copenhagen Interpretation. This basically says a particle can take different states at the same time, for example a particle may be moving or stationary instantaneously. The only way we can know if it is moving, is to measure it. To do so, we would need to use some equipment and interact with it in some way. The very act of measuring will have some effect upon the particle and thus we have determined the outcome of whether it is moving or not. Confused?

To this day, the Copenhagen Interpretation is the most accepted and taught interpretation of quantum mechanics, and yet few beyond the discipline have heard of it. That many more have heard of Schrödinger's cat is testimony to Schrödinger's understanding of both quantum mechanics and the need to express its concepts in a way the world could understand. Admittedly, expressing quantum mechanics in a way the layman can understand is still akin to a YouTube tutorial for brain surgery.

Schrödinger described the following in his work "Die gegenwärtige Situation in der Quantenmechanik (The present situation in quantum mechanics)":

A cat is penned up in a steel chamber, along with the following device (which must be secured against direct interference by the cat): in a Geiger counter, there is a tiny bit of radioactive substance, so small, that perhaps in the course of the hour one of the atoms decays, but also, with equal probability, perhaps none; if it happens, the counter tube discharges and through a relay releases a hammer that shatters a small flask of hydrocyanic acid. If one has left this entire system to itself for an hour, one would say that the cat still lives if meanwhile no atom has decayed. The psi-function of the entire system would express this by having in it the living and dead cat (pardon the expression) mixed or smeared out in equal parts.

To this day, while the Copenhagen Interpretation is accepted, meaning a particle may take two states at once, any application to the "real world" such as in the above is still greatly debated.

Appendix 4: Hypothetical Situations

- If I found out a colleague was stealing company property, what would I do?
- If I was lost in the wilderness, how would I make fire and shelter?
- If I desperately needed money and knew I would not get caught, would I steal?
- If I woke up in a hospital with no memory of my previous life (but complete recall of my current skill set) what would I do?
- If I was told I only had 1 year to live, what would I do? What about 10 years?
- If I could travel back in time and change just one decision in my life, what would it be and would I risk it?
- If I were invisible for 24 hours, how would I spend them? (Be as specific as possible for the whole 24 hours)
- If I were to have a child, and could design it genetically, would I? If I had to design it genetically, what characteristics would I choose and why?
- If I never had to sleep again, how would I use my time?

Appendix 5: Maslow's Hierarchy of Needs

Abraham Maslow first presented his "hierarchy of needs" in his paper *"A Theory of Human Motivation"* in 1943. The basic theory behind this was a stepping stone hierarchy of human needs - the lowest step needing to be fulfilled before the next step could be satisfied. These needs are as follows:

Physiological – Those things needed for survival such as water, food as well as clothing and shelter.

Safety – Safety can be provided in a number of ways and will differ depending on the society a person lives in. For most people this will mean the ability to live their life in relatively good health free from harm. To a lot of people this will mean financial security.

Love – While the search for love is a major part of our lives, these needs can be fulfilled to some extent with close friends and a feeling of community.

Esteem – Different people will feel proud of different achievements, be it through work or personal activity. Most people find their activity has to serve some purpose to have self esteem, be it helping society, or providing for a family.

Self-Actualisation – When we have satisfied all other needs, have we fulfilled our ultimate potential? Being all you can be can provide true contentment in the knowledge you can do no more.

Maslow expanded on his ideas at length in his 1954 book *"Motivation and Personality"*. These ideas are now commonly represented in pyramidal form, although Maslow himself never used such a representation.

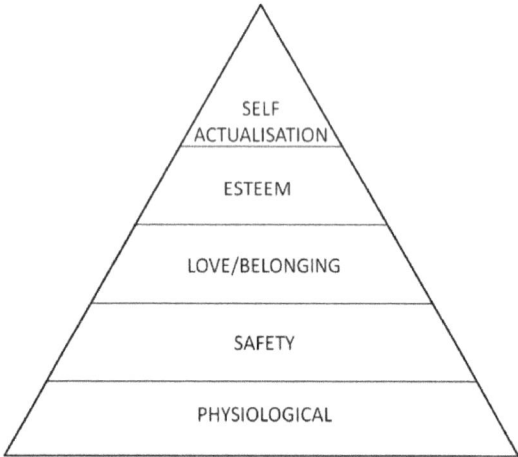

Appendix 6: Comfort Zone Diagram

This appendix contains a blank Comfort Zone diagram that can be photocopied and enlarged for personal use:

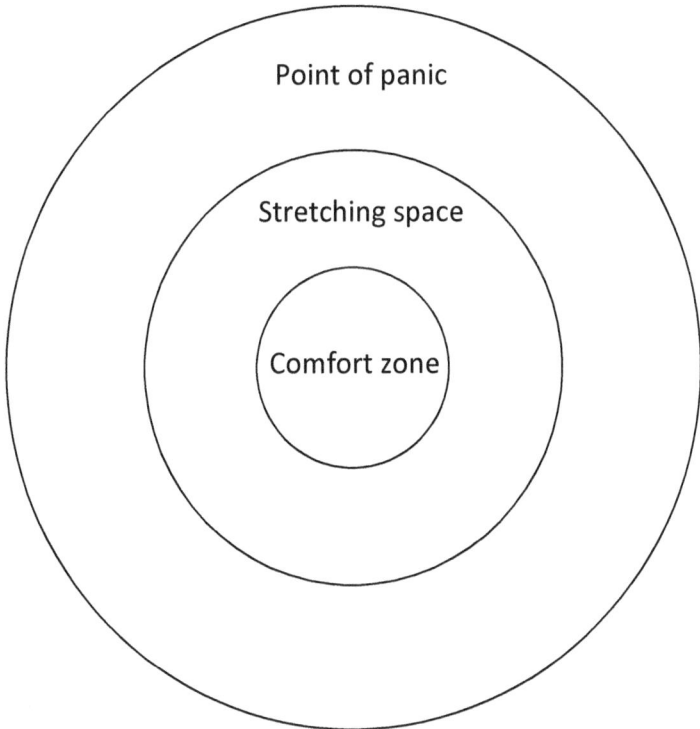

Point of panic

Stretching space

Comfort zone

Appendix 7: Questioning Limiting Beliefs

This appendix contains a blank Questioning Limiting Beliefs diagram that can be photocopied and enlarged for personal use:

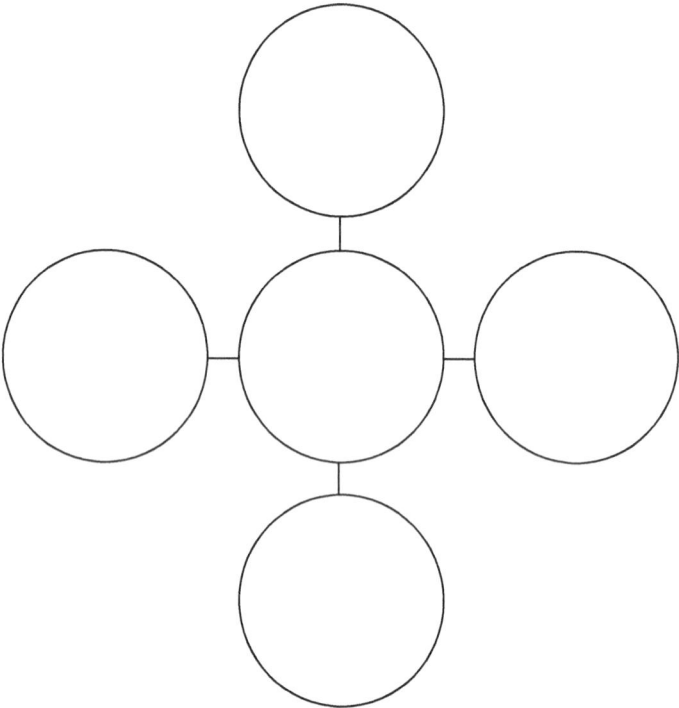

Appendix 8: New Experiences Checklist

o Work in a different part of the office for a day
o Travel home via a different route
o Sleep on the opposite side of the bed
o Get a drink from a café you've never visited
o Speak to a stranger
o Listen to a new radio station
o Eat a food you have never tried before
o Do a new type of exercise
o Speak to a different neighbour
o Donate an item to a different charity
o Read a book (or poem or short story)
o Try a different type of tea (or coffee if you must)
o Get your hair cut in a different barber/salon
o Learn to cook a new dish
o Have different friends round for dinner
o Read a new newspaper or magazine
o Wear a different colour to work
o Try a different hairstyle
o Watch a film you wouldn't normally consider
o Learn one phrase in a new language
o *Write three of your own below*
o
o

Storm in a Teacup?

Acknowledgements

My life changed after several months in and out of York Teaching Hospital. Special thanks must go to the nurses who cared for me during my time there, particularly those who often tended to me through the most painful nights. I am sorry I cannot thank you all by name, but every one of you played a part in my journey. Thanks also to the many doctors whom have played a part in my recovery.

After months in hospital, I quit full time work to follow my passion for coaching and writing. Many people said I was taking a big risk. I personally felt sacrificing 15 hours a day for the next few decades of my life, to pursue happiness in my "old age" was the riskier strategy. Thus it was I found myself with a lot of time on my hands. Over the course of many months of rehabilitation, I often met with my brother to discuss the future. His encouragement was paramount to many wonderful decisions I have made. Also, it was while sat in the 1331 restaurant in York that I had the idea for this publication.

I cannot count the many cups of tea I drank during the writing of this book, but I can recommend the many teahouses and coffee shops I frequented for both inspiration and a quiet place to write. Should you visit the city of York, do find time to visit any of El Piano, The Perky Peacock, Bruks, Mairs and of course the inimitable Betty's found across Yorkshire. Travelling farther afield I would also like to thank Lizzie's Tearooms in Ashby-de-la-Zouch, the very last tearoom I visited before publishing this book.

While on the subject of local companies, there can be few businesses that provide a greater service to the community than a local hairdressing salon. I was fortunate over the many months to get my haircut regularly by Rachel Stead of Revive Hair Design. Whether I was recalling the rather unpleasant details of septicaemia or seeing what the ideas for each chapter actually sounded like when I spoke them aloud, Rach gave the impression of enthrallment, genuine interest and enthusiasm. I strongly encourage people to seek out the services of coaches, counsellors or other types of psychotherapists, but the benefit of simply talking to someone can be reaped with a great hair stylist.

Stylists aside, I have been lucky to work with some fantastic coaches. Some had direct influence over me writing this book, while others have provided general inspiration. I would like to thank

Karin Laudin, Robbie Wils, Julie Miles, Ceylan Sakallioglu and Kris Robertson.

Thanks to the world's greatest marketing manager, Michael Hooley. Your harsh, but constructive feedback was as welcome as the hours spent discussing football.

To all tea drinkers, thank you for every time you offer to make someone a cup. To those like my friends Deb Hughes and Dr. Christine Skinner, every time you invite someone round for tea, you make their life a little better. I have the best neighbours!

Finally, while I dedicated this book to my fiancée, I would also like to thank all the friends who supported me along the way, some with their feedback and others with gentle words of encouragement. Those who have helped me prior to writing this book know who they are: all the boys from school and my good mates from university. The friends who have helped me since I began writing may not realise how big their contribution has been, but without their friendship this book may not have come to fruition: Kate Stead, Thomas Hook, Maxwell King, Gavin Wadsworth, Christine Bennett, Alice Osborne, Dr Bryony Richards-McClung, Johanna Hoffert and Hendrik Müller, I thank you all.

Bibliography

Covey, Stephen R. *The 7 Habits of Highly Effective People*. Simon Schuster 2001.

The Dalai Lama. *A Profound Mind*. Hodder & Staughton 2011

Dweck, Carol. *Mindset: How you can fulfil your potential*. Robinson 2012

Elder, Zoë. *Full On Learning*. Crown House 2012

Gladwell, Michael. *The Tipping Point: How Little Things Can Make a Big Difference*. Little, Brown and Company, 2000

Gladwell, Michael. *Outliers: The Story of Success*. Penguin 2009

Grayling, A. C. *The Good Book*. Bloomsbury 2013

Grylls, Bear. *A Survival Guide for Life*. Bantam Press 2012.

Haig, Matt. *Reasons to Stay Alive.* Canongate Books 2015

Harrold, Fiona. *Be Your Own Life Coach: How to take control of your life and live your wildest dreams.* Hodder Paperbacks 2001

James, Bev. *Do it! Or Ditch it.* Virgin Books 2011

Johnson, Dr Spencer. *Who Moved My Cheese?* Vermillion 1999

Landsberg, Max. *The Tao of Coaching.* Profile Books, 2015

Lundin, Stephen, Ph.D., Harry Paul and John Christensen. *Fish.* Hodder & Staughton 2011

Maslow, Abraham. *Motivation and Personality.* Harper Brothers, 1954

Millman, Dan. *Way of the Peaceful Warrior.* HJ Kramer 2000

Orwell, George. "A Nice Cup of Tea" *Evening Standard*, 12 January 1946

Rhodes, James. *Instrumental.* Canongate Books, 2015

Schrödinger, Erwin. "Die gegenwärtige Situation in der Quantenmechanik (The present situation in quantum mechanics)". *Naturwissenschaften* 23 (48): 807–812, November 1935

Syed, Matthew. *Bounce: The Myth of Talent and the Power of Practice.* Fourth Estate 2011

Thomas, Eric. *The Secret of Success.* Eric Thomas 2013

Tolle, Eckhart. *The Power of Now.* Hodder & Staughton 2011

Tzu, Lao. *Tao Te Ching* (translated by Stephen Mitchell). Frances Lincoln 1999

Watkins, Michael. *The first 90 days: Critical success strategies for new leaders at all levels.* Harvard Business Review Press 2013

www.ingramcontent.com/pod-product-compliance
Lightning Source LLC
Chambersburg PA
CBHW071816020426
42331CB00007B/1506